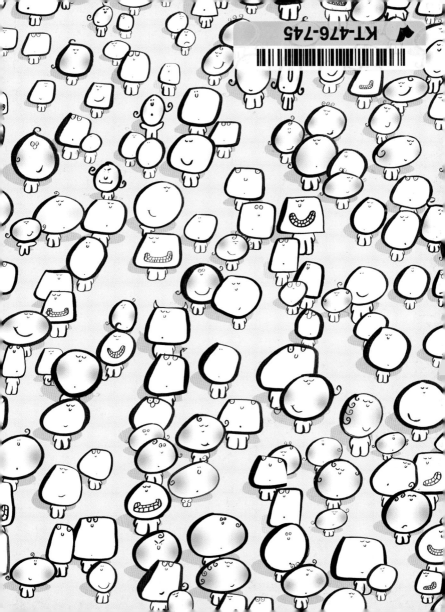

mums

with Vimrod

mums

behind
every
great
woman
is her
bum

Vimrod by Lisa Swerling and Ralph Lazar

HarperCollins*Publishers*

i reckon you're the **best** mum i ever had

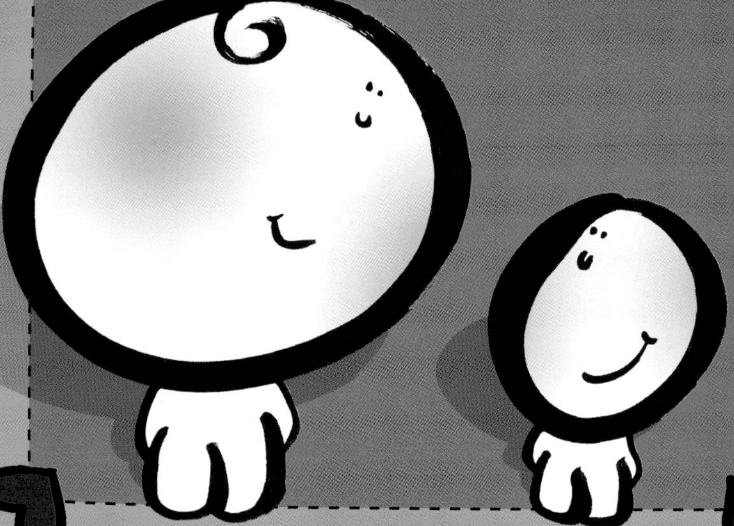

my mum
can juggle so many things at once

that she keeps getting headhunted
by the moscow state circus

on the station platform of life, my mum is the dream vending machine that dispenses crisps and sweets and other nice things for free.

if it weren't for my mum, my life would fall apart. she's like wood glue really.

mum, you are better than **all** other mums in the **history** of **mumness.**

other mums

the prime minister of india

gave my mum an award for her contribution to his country's economy.

i think she drinks too much tea.

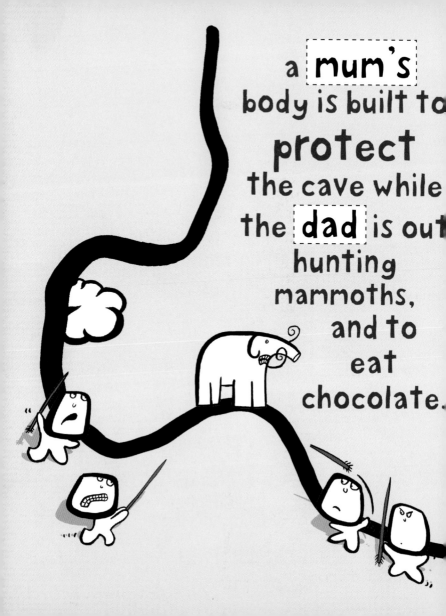

a **mum's** body is built to **protect** the cave while the **dad** is out hunting mammoths, and to eat chocolate.

i don't believe in god but i do believe that some being or force created mums.

definitely.

once a spider was
rude to my mum,
and since that day,
i have always disliked
spiders.

no-one, i repeat, no-one,
is rude to my mum.

mum, i know it was a long time ago, but thanks for all that breast milk, it was really delicious.

if we lived in hollywood

i have no doubt that brad pitt,
russell crowe and tom cruise
(amongst others)
would be continually
trying to climb over our wall
so they could spend time with
my mum.

mum, in the rich pageant of life

you are the fulcrum, the spigot, the ratchet and the gasket,

i.e. you are important and great and sensible.

extraordinary!

my mum takes **life** as it comes,

i.e. in small chunks
that are shaped like chocolate,
taste like chocolate and
most likely are chocolate...

YuM! YuM! YUM!

i dunno what it's like now,
but my mum's womb
was **super cool**
back then.

lisa swerling + ralph lazar
are two of the UK's most familiar
graphic artists. Through their company
Last Lemon they have spawned a catwalk
of popular cartoon characters, which
includes Harold's Planet, The Brainwaves,
Blessthischick and, of course, Vimrod.

Writers, artists and designers, they are
married with two children, and spend
their time between London and various
beaches on the Indian Ocean.

HarperCollins*Publishers*

77–85 Fulham Palace Road, Hammersmith, London W6 8JB

www.harpercollins.co.uk

Published by HarperCollins*Publishers* 2007

1

A catalogue record for this book is available from the British Library

ISBN-10   0 00 724207 7
ISBN-13   978 0 00 724207 8

Set in Bokka

Printed and bound in Italy by Lego SpA

other titles in the Vimrod collection:

drink!
Wine is made to be drunk, I am drunk, therefore am i wine?

Vimrod by Lisa Swerling and Ralph Lazar

shopping
it's the little voices that tell me to go shopping

Vimrod by Lisa Swerling & Ralph Lazar

farting
my farts hospitalise small children

Vimrod by Lisa Swerling & Ralph Lazar

xmas
christmas is coming run!

Vimrod by Lisa Swerling & Ralph Lazar

chocolate
life is a struggle between good, evil and chocolate

Vimrod by Lisa Swerling & Ralph Lazar

dads
life is a journey between the fridge and the sofa

Vimrod by Lisa Swerling and Ralph Lazar

love
you and me... ...two hamsters on the spinning-wheel of life

Vimrod by Lisa Swerling and Ralph Lazar

(watch this space)

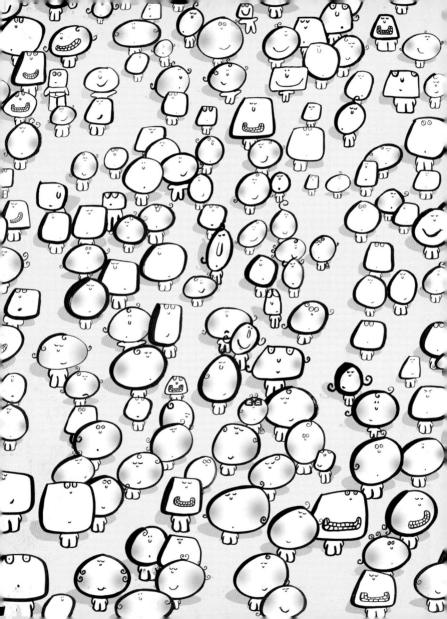